Dark Enough to See the STARS

STUDY GUIDE

Cindy Noonan

High Star Press

Dark Enough to See the Stars Study Guide
Copyright 2020 by Cindy Noonan
Published by High Star Press

High Star Press LLC
1143 Northern Blvd. # 307
Clarks Summit, PA 18411

All rights reserved. No part of this book may be reproduced, stored in a retrieval system, or transmitted in any form or by any means-electronic, mechanical, photocopy, recording, or otherwise-without prior written permission of the copyright owner, Front cover imagery from www.oldbike.edu.

Cover design and interior layout design by Cathy Sanders. www.csbookdesign.com

ISBN: 978-0-9981808-2-3

Contents

Dark Enough to See the Stars in a Nutshell	5
The Times in Which Moses Lived	7
Before You Read the Book	11
Glossary	13
Chapters 1 - 4	15
Chapters 5 - 8	19
Chapters 9 - 12	23
Chapters 13 - 18	27
Chapters 19 - 23	31
Chapters 24 - 30	35
Chapters 31 - 34	39
Chapters 35 - 38	43
Underground Railroad and Dark Enough to See the Stars Exam	49
Dark Enough to See the Stars Answer Key	55

Dark Enough to See the Stars in a Nutshell

Dark Enough to See the Stars is the story of Moses, a twelve-year-old slave who resolves to escape from his plantation in Maryland and seek freedom in the North. Moses' mother has often told him that he won't be a slave forever. She believes that someday he will run away and help other slaves to freedom. She teaches him to follow the North Star and hopes to see her dream fulfilled.

At the beginning of the story, Moses' mother learns she has been sold to a plantation in the Deep South. Moses says, "If they is gonna rip me away from her like seed outta cotton, then I'm gonna be free." Moses and his mother plan his escape. While everyone watches his mother board a train with other slaves who have been sold, Moses flees into the woods. Although grief-stricken, he takes comfort in knowing that his mama will be happy if he is free.

Moses finds his way to a miller who is known to hide slaves on the Underground Railroad. The miller helps Moses travel north until he reaches Harrisburg, Pennsylvania, where Reverend Palmer and his wife give him shelter. He spends several weeks there helping with chores. Another runaway slave, Tillie, who has lived with the Palmers several years, teaches him the alphabet, and Mrs. Palmer gives him reading lessons.

At this time, however, Congress passes the Fugitive Slave Act of 1850 and slaves living in free states are no longer safe. Anyone caught assisting a slave in any way will be fined a thousand dollars per slave and be sentenced to six months in jail. This means that Moses and Tillie must leave. The Palmers make plans for their safe passage to Canada, but before they can get out, the local sheriff and his men invade the house at night. Moses and Tillie escape out the back door.

They follow a canal path north and are rescued by Daniel Hughes, a half-black, half-Indian canal boat captain who takes them on his barge to Williamsport. However, his hired man, Jeb, makes advances toward Tillie. Moses punches Jeb in the nose and vows he won't let him touch Tillie again.

Moses and Tillie continue to find people who are willing to risk their lives to help them. An Indian leads them through the woods to Elmira, New York. A steamboat captain in Ithaca transports them across Cayuga Lake.

While on the boat, Tillie sees something that horrifies her. Jeb has followed them. They hide in the storage hold until the boat docks. Then they sneak onto a train and ride to Rochester, where they meet black abolitionist and newspaperman, Frederick Douglass.

Douglass' employee Joseph drives Moses and Tillie to his home in a horse and buggy. Just as they arrive, two men on horseback confront them at gunpoint. One of them is Jeb. The other is a black man named Aaron. Moses is angry and appalled that a black man would betray his own people. Joseph slides the reins next to Moses and gets off the carriage. He tells Jeb and Aaron they will talk about turning the runaways in if Jeb puts away his gun. As he does so, Joseph swats the horse. Moses grabs the reins as the mare takes off at a gallop. Bullets fly around them, but Moses and Tillie keep going. Other shots are fired, and Moses hears someone yell, "He's dead!" Having no idea who might have died, Moses and Tillie keep going until they reach a stagecoach company in Lockport, New York. The horse has taken them to his former home and owner.

Moses and Tillie tell T.W. Fanning, who owns the business, how Jeb, Aaron, or—worse yet—Joseph may have died. Fanning makes plans to hide Moses and Tillie in the mailbags on top of a stagecoach and send them to Canada across the bridge on the Niagara River. Dan, one of Fanning's workers, overhears the plans. No one knows that he is Aaron's brother. Dan convinces Mr. Fanning that slavers are riding the next stage and encourages him to wait until the next day to send Moses and Tillie. Meanwhile, he surreptitiously rides to Rochester to find out if his brother is dead.

When Dan goes missing, Fanning realizes Dan lied to him. Everyone hopes Dan doesn't return. The next day Moses and Tillie ride the stage to Niagara without a problem. The weather is chilly, and the mist rising from the gorge below ices up the bridge. As they walk across to Canada, they hear horses galloping toward them. Jeb and Dan are in pursuit. Tillie slips on the bridge, and Moses tries to help her. Jeb lassoes her from his horse and ties her to his arm. Dan's horse slips on the bridge, and Dan gets pinned underneath. Although Moses could escape, he refuses to leave Tillie. As Jeb turns toward Moses to tie him up, Tillie leaps over the bridge, dragging Jeb with her. They fall to their deaths in the Niagara Gorge.

With the help of the bridge toll keeper, Moses makes it to Canada. He is distraught over Tillie's death, knowing that she sacrificed her life so he could be free. He finds lodging with black abolitionist Henry Bibb and attends school at the Bibb's school for runaways. He hopes to become an abolitionist writer like Henry Bibb and Frederick Douglass.

He writes his mother a letter, which the Bibbs print in their newspaper. Moses hopes to find her someday. He is thankful for her encouragement and prayers and the help and prayers of all the people, black and white, who risked their lives for his freedom, especially Tillie.

The Times in Which Moses Lived

The Slave Trade

Slavery has existed for thousands of years. It was practiced by every major ancient civilization. For a variety of reasons, prisoners of war, indebted people, and criminals were made slaves. Children could also be sold into slavery by their parents to pay a debt.

The Middle East, Africa, China, and even Europe condoned slavery in the 1600s. African tribes often sold prisoners from rival tribes into slavery. While Europeans were colonizing America, slave traders were buying people in western Africa and transporting them across the Atlantic Ocean. Between ten to fifteen million slaves were shipped to the New World. Most were sent to the West Indies, Central America, and South America. Over 300,000 arrived in the American colonies.

The first Africans, purchased from Spanish slave traders, arrived in America at the Jamestown Colony in 1619. At first, Africans were often treated as indentured servants whose service was considered payment for their freedom. However, this practice dwindled as the demand for cheap labor on plantations increased.

By 1700, most American colonies had legalized slavery. However, in 1777, Vermont banned slavery from its constitution, and by 1804, the anti-slavery movement had succeeded in passing legislation prohibiting slavery in the North. Congress banned the import or export of slaves from international ports in 1808, but slaves could still be bought and sold within the United States. Children born to slaves were considered slaves. Families were often split apart as children and parents were sold to different owners.

The Abolition Movement

In 1688, Quakers at the Society of Friends Meetinghouse in Germantown, Philadelphia, presented the first petition advocating abolishment of slavery. The document was ignored for 150 years but was rediscovered in 1844. Abolitionists, many of whom were Quakers and Methodists, disagreed with slavery on religious grounds, declaring that the United States Constitution stated that all men were created equal. They referred to the early petition first presented by Quakers who wanted to abolish slavery. Pennsylvania passed the Gradual Abolition Act in 1780, becoming the first Northern state to write laws governing the emancipation of slaves. All children born of slaves were considered free men but served as indentured servants until age twenty-eight. By 1847, no slaves were listed in Pennsylvania records. Other Northern states followed, many granting immediate emancipation.

When slaves learned about freedom in the North, they often escaped and traveled north. The routes, homes, businesses and people that assisted them soon became known as the Underground Railroad. People risked their lives to help runaways, often facing hostile neighbors who disagreed with their stance on slavery or who preferred to wait and see if legislation would pass granting freedom. Many felt abolitionist radical beliefs would upset the fragile economy and take jobs from whites. They also feared that these uneducated, unskilled workers would be problematic in society.

The Fugitive Slave Act of 1850

The Fugitive Slave Act of 1850 was passed on September 18th as a part of the Compromise of 1850. This law attempted to settle differences between the slave and free states concerning the status of territories acquired during the Mexican-American War. As part of that law, the Fugitive Slave Act required law enforcement in the North to assist in the return of escaped slaves to their masters. Formerly, Northerners ignored requests to return slaves and often helped them escape. The law stated that any official who did not cooperate was subject to a $1,000 fine (the equivalent of $29,000 today). Anyone who aided a slave in his or her quest for freedom had to pay the fine and spend six months in jail. No proof of purchase was necessary, and slaves had no rights in a court of law. This ruling, voted on by Congress, angered Northerners. The lack of necessary proof also led to the capture of many free blacks who were returned to slavery. This attempt to appease the South only galvanized the North's position. Many who had been neutral or indifferent subsequently supported emancipation.

The Civil War and the Emancipation Proclamation

The issue of slavery was a major factor that led the South to secede from the Union, inciting the Civil War. In response to the South's rebellion, Abraham Lincoln issued the Emancipation Proclamation on January 1, 1863. Lincoln gave this executive order under his authority as Commander in Chief of the armed forces. It was issued after a series of warnings allowing Southern Confederate supporters sixty days to surrender to avoid confiscation of land and slaves. It changed the federal status of slaves to freemen in all states that seceded. As soon as Union troops captured an area, slaves were released. Since this was a war measure, the following slave states that did not leave the Union were not subject to this law: Kentucky, Maryland, Delaware, and Missouri. West Virginia joined them later after separating from Virginia. After the war, on December 18, 1865, the thirteenth amendment to the constitution was adopted which abolished slavery, except as punishment for a crime.

Frederick Douglass

Frederick Douglass was born sometime in February of 1818 under the name of Frederick Augustus Washington Bailey. Slaves were often unaware of their exact birthdate, because they were rarely recorded. He escaped from slavery in Maryland and soon became active in Massachusetts and New York as an abolitionist, writer, and speaker. He changed his name to Frederick Douglass to emphasize his new identity as a free person. Slaveholders often argued that slaves weren't intelligent enough to function independently in society as citizens. Douglass' gifted ability to write and speak in a scholarly manner countered the prevailing opinions of the day. He wrote several autobiographies, including *Narrative of the Life of Frederick Douglass, An American Slave,* which became a bestseller, *My Bondage and My Freedom,* and *Life and Times of Frederick Douglass,* which he penned after the Civil War.

Douglass spent time traveling and speaking in Ireland and England. Upon returning to the United States in 1847, he published his first newspaper, the *North Star*, in Rochester, New York. The *North Star's* motto was "Right is of no sex—Truth is of no color—God is the father of us all, and we are all brethren." Douglass also supported the Women's Suffrage movement. After the Civil War, he continued to champion equal rights for African-Americans and for women.

He died on February 20, 1895 from a massive heart attack at the age of seventy-seven. He had just returned from a meeting of the National Council of Women, where he had received a standing ovation.

Henry Bibb

Henry Bibb was born on May 10, 1815 to Mildred Jackson, a slave on a Kentucky plantation. He was told his father was James Bibb, a white Kentucky state senator, a man Henry never knew. He had six brothers who were all sold to other slaveholders. He married another slave, Malinda, in 1833. Five years later, Henry fled to Canada but returned to Kentucky to try to free his wife. She had been sold to a white planter who made her his mistress, and she did not want to travel to Canada. Henry was captured and sold to gamblers, but he managed to escape and flee north to Detroit in December of 1840. He then concentrated on his career as an abolitionist, traveling and lecturing in the free states. Around 1850 he published his autobiography, *Narrative of the Life and Adventures of Henry Bibb, an American Slave.* This became a well-known and well-respected slave narrative which criticized the institution of slavery and gave insight into Southern plantation culture. However, when the Fugitive Slave Act of 1850 passed, he and his second wife, Mary, fled to Canada because fugitive slaves were no longer safe in the Northern states.

In 1851, he established the first black newspaper in Canada called *The Voice of the Fugitive.* This newspaper helped build sympathy among Canadians for the slaves' plight and also offered advice to incoming fugitives. Because of his fame as an author, three of his brothers who later escaped were reunited with him. He died at the age of thirty-nine in 1854.

Thaddeus Stevens

Stevens was born April 14, 1792, to poor parents in rural Vermont. He had a clubfoot, which caused him to limp his entire life. As a young man, he moved to Pennsylvania and practiced law in Gettysburg. He was elected to the Pennsylvania House of Representatives and later joined the Whig Party. He was elected to the United States Congress in 1848, however, his strong views opposing slavery lost him votes, and he didn't run for office in 1852. He ran again and was elected in 1858 under the newly formed Republican Party. Stevens and others like him were known as the Radical Republicans. They opposed Congress' plans to expand slavery. When the war erupted, he played an important role in financing it through taxes and borrowed money. He believed not only that slaves should be freed, but also that land should be confiscated from plantation owners and given to slaves, a highly disputed idea.

After the war and Lincoln's assassination, Stevens led the Radical Republicans in opposing President Andrew Johnson's plans for restoring the seceded states, particularly because they offered little restitution or guarantee of rights to the freed slaves. He led the Republicans in seeking to remove Johnson in an unsuccessful impeachment trial.

Although in his seventies with failing health, Stevens continued to champion the rights of blacks with limited success. Except for his legislation that established free public schools in Pennsylvania, he considered his life a failure. He died at home on August 11, 1868, surrounded by his friends and family. He chose to be buried in Lancaster, Pennsylvania, and composed his own epitaph, "I repose in this quiet and secluded spot, not for any natural preference for solitude. But finding other cemeteries limited as to race by charter rules, I have chosen this that I might illustrate in my death the principles which I advocated through a long life, equality of man before his creator."

At the turn of the twentieth century, historians viewed Stevens as an angry, reckless man who hated white Southerners. By the 1950s, he was praised for his progressive views on racial equality that were before his time.

Before You Read the Book

1. Read the title and look at the cover. What do you think the story will be about? Have you read other books about slavery or the Underground Railroad? Were they fiction or nonfiction?

2. *Dark Enough to See the Stars* is a work of historical fiction. What is the difference between a non-fiction book and an historical novel?

3. What is the advantage of reading historical fiction?

4. Discuss in a group what other works of historical fiction you have read. What period in history was covered? Which historical characters did you learn about? We can learn from studying our past. How does learning about history impact what we believe?

5. Take a look at the map on page nine. Through which states did Moses travel? How many miles did he travel? How long do you think it took him to reach Canada?

Glossary

Drinking Gourd:
A phrase used by slaves to describe the Big Dipper, which pointed to the North Star.

Promised Land:
A term for the Promised Land of the Jews, also eventually called Israel, which they reached after slavery in Egypt. Used by slaves to describe the North or Canada, where they could reach freedom.

Overseer:
A taskmaster who supervised field slaves.

Carpetbag:
A suitcase made of carpet and used for traveling.

Ashcake:
A pancake made out of cornmeal and water and cooked over an open fire.

Tow Linen:
Coarse, heavy linen made from short fibers and used to make clothing in the 18th and 19th centuries.

Mason-Dixon Line:
Two surveyors named Mason and Dixon surveyed the boundary between Maryland and Pennsylvania in the 1700s. Before the Civil War, this boundary line defined the separation of slave states from free states. It still refers to the division between the North and South.

Chapters 1 - 4

DIALECT

Dialect is a regional variety of speech that differs from the normal usage of a language in pronunciation, grammar, and vocabulary. I have used dialect and slang to make my characters seem more realistic. You can find the following words in the first chapter of the book. Fill in the blanks with what you think each dialect or slang word or phrase means.

1. So's _____
2. Gonna _____
3. Ain't _____
4. Goin' _____
5. Outta _____
6. Catched _____
7. Knowed _____
8. Growed _____
9. Masta _____
10. Whupped _____
11. Gits _____
12. Forgit _____
13. Jus' _____

Vocabulary:

Write the letter of the definition next to the correct vocabulary word.

1. ___ Kindling	A. Fire-lighting material
2. ___ Bulrush	B. Boyfriend
3. ___ Cowcatcher	C. Arguing
4. ___ Depot	D. To shape wood by carving
5. ___ Ruckus	E. A traveling pot mender
6. ___ Gully	F. Crying
7. ___ Lash	G. A ditch or channel made for water
8. ___ Beau	H. To strike with a whip
9. ___ Whittling	I. A person who helped slaves go from one safe place to another
10. ___ Squabbling	J. A fight
11. ___ Tinker	K. A device on a train engine used to remove obstructions from the tracks
12. ___ Conductor	
13. ___ Yowling	L. Grass-like marsh plant
14. ___ Agent	M. A train station
	N. A coordinator who planned how slaves would escape

Dark Enough to See the Stars Study Guide

Fill in the blanks:

Find a word from the box below to use in each sentence.

1. Austin and Alexa were _____ over whose turn it was to set the table for dinner.

2. The scouts searched for _____ to start a campfire.

3. We picked up our sister from Chicago at the train _____.

4. My baby brother started _____ when I accidently stepped on his toe.

5. The soccer players started a _____ when they thought the referee made a bad call.

6. The _____ filled up with rainwater after the storm.

7. The train's _____ pushed some branches off the train track.

8. My uncle carved a walking stick with his _____ knife.

9. Austin teased Alexa and said the new boy in her class was her _____.

10. Harriet Tubman was a _____ on the Underground Railroad, taking slaves to freedom in the North.

11. An _____ for the Underground Railroad told Moses' mama how and where he could escape.

Kindling	Bulrush	Cowcatcher	Depot
Ruckus	Gully	Lash	Beau
Whittling	Squabbling	Tinker	Conductor
	Yowling	Agent	

Story Questions:

1. Why did Moses' mother name him after Moses in the Bible?

_____

2. What was the Drinking Gourd? _____

3. Why was Moses worried when Zeke followed him?

_____

4. What kind of work did Moses' mama do on the plantation?

_____

5. A skunk sprayed the slave catchers' dogs. How did this help Moses?

_____

6. How did Moses feel when he met Joel?

_____

Dark Enough to See the Stars Study Guide

Discussion Questions:

1. If you were Moses, would you have chosen to run away? Why or why not?

_____

_____

_____

2. What do you think it felt like to be owned by somebody?

_____

_____

_____

3. Describe a day in the life of a slave. How is it different from your day?

_____

_____

_____

Science connection:

1. Watch a YouTube video about how to locate the North Star. https://www.youtube.com/watch?v=Mopqp9XtO0M

2. Draw the Big Dipper and North Star on a folder. Use it to store your worksheets.

3. Fun facts:

    A. The North Star is also called Polaris.

    B. Slaves named the Big Dipper the Drinking Gourd. The Indians called it Great Bear. In England it is known as the Plough.

    C. The Big Dipper is not a constellation; rather it is a pattern of stars called an asterism.

Literary Devices:

1. *Point of View*—this term refers to the individual telling the story. Is a character in the book narrating (first person), or is the author (third person)?

    - Who is telling this story? _____

    - Why do you think the author chose this point of view?

    _____

2. *Personification*—the author or character in the book attributes a human quality to an inanimate object.

- Moses said the water wheel at the mill wasn't thirsty because it kept dumping water back into the river. What human characteristic does Moses give the wheel?

___

- Why do you think the author uses this device? What other examples of personification can you find?

___

___

Social Studies Connection:

Understanding the Impact of Slavery.

1. Parents and teachers, read the following blog from Oxford University Press: "Slavery: A Dehumanizing Institution." https://blog.oup.com/2006/02/slavery_a_dehum/

2. Discuss the psychological affects of separation from families, extreme physical punishment, or watching family members being punished.

Writing Activity:

Write about a time you were separated from a family member. How did it make you feel? Was the situation resolved? How?

Or write a paragraph using personification of an inanimate object.

___

___

___

___

___

___

___

Chapters 5 - 8

Vocabulary:

Write the letter of the definition next to the correct vocabulary word.

1. ___ Hitched	A. A type of paint, also means to cover up
2. ___ Hopper	B. Fastened two things together
3. ___ Burlap	C. Old-fashioned word for mattress, a mattress cover
4. ___ Whitewash	D. A rough cloth
5. ___ Hunkered	E. Corn meal mush
6. ___ Grits	F. Food
7. ___ Vittles	G. A funnel-shaped dispenser
8. ___ Tick	H. Crouched or stooped
9. ___ Impudent	I. Disrespectful

Vocabulary:

Find a word from the box below to use in each sentence.

1. The farmer filled the _____ sack with corn.

2. Austin said the _____ were very tasty.

3. The soldier _____ down behind the bush so the enemy couldn't see him.

4. The teacher said that the student who talked back to her was _____.

5. The man painted his front porch with _____.

6. Austin's favorite breakfast is eggs and bacon with _____.

7. The farmer _____ the horse to the wagon.

8. The farmer poured corn in the _____ to grind it into corn meal.

Grits	Hunkered	Whitewash	Burlap
Hopper	Impudent	Vittles	Hitched

Story Questions:

1. Why was Moses afraid of the millstones?

_____

Dark Enough to See the Stars Study Guide

2. Where was Miller Johnson taking Moses? How was he getting there? Why did he have to hide?

_____

3. How did Moses describe each letter that made up his name?

_____

_____

4. What did Daniel Morgan do to the cat and why?

_____

_____

5. Why did Moses scratch his name in the loft floor with a rock?

_____

Discussion Questions:

1. Why do you think Moses had never held a fork before? What else could he have used?

_____

_____

2. Why was Moses uncomfortable when Miller Johnson looked him in the eye? Why do you think slaves weren't allowed to look their masters in the eye?

_____

_____

3. Why do you think slaves weren't allowed to learn to read, and free blacks were even discouraged from doing so?

_____

_____

4. Slaves were often called names that made them feel worthless. Have you ever been called a bad name? How did that make you feel?

_____

_____

_____

Literary Devices:

1. *Simile*—A simile is a figure of speech comparing one object to another using the words *like* or *as*. This device is used to better illustrate a description.

> On page 31, Moses thinks the millstones were rocks that "looked like big wheels." He also thought they were "hitched together like two horses to a wagon."

2. *Metaphor*—A metaphor is a figure of speech in which one object is compared to another by speaking as if it were that object. It is like a simile, but doesn't use the words *like* or *as*.

> On page 32 Moses says the millstones "wasn't horses hitched together. They was two big lips smacking."

Writing Activity:

Write one sentence using a metaphor and one sentence using a simile.

_____

_____

_____

Literary Elements

Characterization—The reader learns about the book's characters through the author's description of what they say and do, and by what others say about them. Joel brings food to Moses in the barn loft and teaches him how to write his name. Compare Moses and Joel using the following Venn diagram. Write their common characteristics in the overlapping part of the circle.

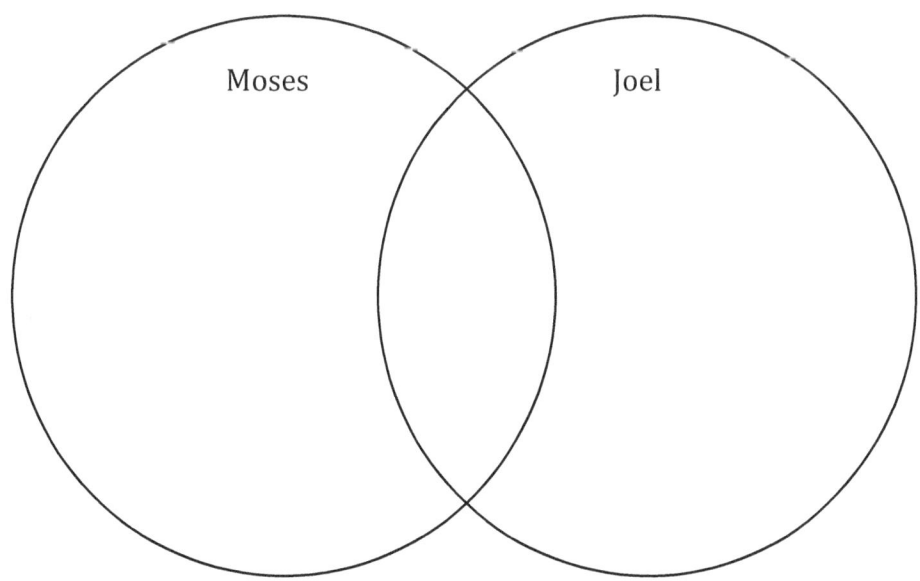

Writing Activity

Based on your Venn diagram, write a paragraph that compares the characteristics of Moses and Joel.

Chapters 9 - 12

Vocabulary:

Write the letter of the definition next to the correct vocabulary word.

1. ___ Mosey	A. Drawing breath in a noisy manner
2. ___ Buckboard	B. To wander about leisurely
3. ___ Flatbed	C. A handkerchief or scarf
4. ___ Bandanna	D. Relatives
5. ___ Kinfolk	E. A trailer with a flat platform without sides
6. ___ Snuffling	F. People who actively opposed slavery in the US
7. ___ Abolitionist	G. A horse-drawn vehicle or carriage having a long, flexible board instead of a body and springs

Vocabulary:

Use a word from the box below to replace the underlined word or phrase in each sentence. Write your answer on the line provided.

1. The children left the playground and strolled up to the house to finish their chores. _____

2. The farmer helped his wife onto the carriage, and they drove into town. _____

3. The men loaded fresh cut lumber on the trailer. _____

4. Alexa's mom tied a scarf around her hair to keep it from blowing in the wind. _____

5. Many people who disagreed with slavery hid people on the Underground Railroad. _____

6. Austin said his relatives from Alabama were coming for a visit. _____

7. Alexa's baby brother was breathing noisily because he had a cold. _____

| Snuffling | Moseyed | Abolitionists | Flatbed |
| Buckboard | Bandanna | Kinfolk | |

Dark Enough to See the Stars Study Guide

Story Questions

1. What was different about the wagon in which Moses was going to ride?

2. Where was Miller Johnson taking Moses?

3. What line were they crossing, and why was that important?

4. Where was the "hidey-hole" in the Dobbin House?

5. Who was Thaddeus Stevens and what did he write for Moses?

6. Did Moses have to hide in the wagon when Henry drove him to Harrisburg? Why or why not?

Discussion Questions:

1. Miller Johnson said he was a "law-abiding man," but he didn't tell the slave catchers that Moses was hiding in the wagon. Why?

2. Thaddeus Stevens wrote Moses a fake free paper to help him escape to Canada. Do you think Thaddeus Stevens was breaking the law?
_____

3. Miller Johnson and Thaddeus Stevens didn't tell the truth about something because they wanted to help Moses. Were they right or wrong? Why?
_____
_____

Literary Device: Imagery

Imagery is a term used in literature to describe scenes that appeal to our five senses. Images that explain something we *see* help readers create pictures in their minds. *Smell, touch, taste, hearing, and seeing* can also be used to characterize a scene. Which senses does the author use in the following examples of imagery?

1. "I took a deep breath. Bacon. I liked that smell a heap better than the hay and horse manure I been sniffing for the last two days." _____

2. "I ran my fingers over my name one last time." _____

3. "I felt sweat drip between my eyes and down my nose." _____

4. "Mr. Dobbin introduced us to his wife, Abigail, who stood at the wood stove stirring a pot. A couple of young 'uns clung on her skirt. A turkey was strung up from the rafter just above me." _____
_____

Social Studies Connection: The Dobbin House

The Dobbin House was an actual stop on the Underground Railroad in Gettysburg. Built in 1776, the house now operates as a restaurant. The hidden room in the staircase is available for tourists to see. Go to http://www.dobbinhouse.com to find out more. Better yet, plan a trip!

Writing Activity:

Imagine that you are Moses hiding in either the wagon or the Dobbin House. Using images that appeal to the senses, describe your experience.
_____
_____
_____
_____

Chapters 13 - 18

Vocabulary:

Write the letter of the definition next to the correct vocabulary word.

1. ___ Hightail	A. To utter loud cries of excitement
2. ___ Clack	B. A group of citizens trained as soldiers, but only called to service in emergencies
3. ___ Whoop	
4. ___ Clomp	C. A path alongside a canal used by mules to pull barges
5. ___ Militia	D. To place or throw something heavily
6. ___ Brandish	E. To make quick, sharp sounds by striking or cracking
7. ___ Plunk	F. Furniture used to hold plates, cups and silverware
8. ___ Sideboard	G. To avoid someone or something by a sudden change of position
9. ___ Dodge	H. To leave quickly
10. ___ Gumption	I. Courage, guts
11. ___ Towpath	J. Stomp or plod
	K. To shake or wave a weapon

Vocabulary:

Find a word from the box below to use in each sentence.

1. Alexa and Austin _____ it out of the park when it started to rain.
2. The mule pulled the barge through the canal as it trod up the_____.
3. Alexa _____ four quarters on the table to pay for the chewing gum.
4. The Spanish dancer _____ her castanets in rhythm to the music.
5. Austin didn't have the _____ to jump off the high dive.
6. Mom put the dishes away in the _____.
7. The pirates _____ their swords as they fought to take the ship's treasure.
8. Many states formed _____ to protect themselves during the Revolutionary War.
9. As Alexa sat in the bleachers, she _____ the fly ball that headed toward her.
10. The team _____ with excitement when they learned they made the playoffs.
11. Austin _____ through the kitchen with his muddy boots.

Hightailed	Clacked	Whooped	Clomped
Militias	Brandished	Plunked	Sideboard
Dodged	Gumption	Towpath	

Dark Enough to See the Stars Study Guide

Story Questions

1. What was ruined when Henry and Moses were caught in a rainstorm?

2. Tillie and Mrs. Palmer convinced the reverend to let Moses live with them for a while. What did they say to convince him?

3. What was the punishment for helping slaves according to the Fugitive Slave Act?

4. What did Moses want to be when he grew up?

5. Why did Moses and Tillie have to leave?

Discussion Questions

1. Dr. Rutherford said that even free blacks weren't always treated right by lawmen. Why did he say that?

2. The Fugitive Slave Act was written to try to ease tensions between the North and South. Do you think it accomplished its purpose? Why or why not?

3. Learning to read, write, and get an education is important for people to succeed. Why is this true?

4. Moses thanked God for a stinking outhouse. Why? Can something that seems bad turn out for the good?

_____

_____

_____

_____

_____

_____

_____

Literary Elements: Conflict

Conflict happens when two opposing forces struggle against one another. When a character fights against nature, a community, or a person, it is called *external conflict*. When someone struggles with his or her own thoughts it is called *internal conflict*. List some of the conflicts that have happened in the story so far. Have any of them been resolved? If so, how?

_____

_____

_____

_____

_____

_____

_____

_____

_____

Writing Activity:
Write about a conflict, internal or external, that you have experienced and tell how it was resolved or how you think it might be resolved.

Internal Conflicts   **Resolutions**

External Conflicts   **Resolutions**

Chapters 19 - 23

Vocabulary:

Write the letter of the definition next to the correct vocabulary word.

1. ___ Draft Animal	A. To argue
2. ___ Bicker	B. An animal used to pull heavy loads
3. ___ Acquaintance	C. The part of a canal that contains gates used for opening or closing and for control of the water level. It allows boats to pass from one water level to another.
4. ___ Lock	
5. ___ Lock House	
6. ___ Sizzle	D. A person known to you but not a close friend or someone you meet for the first time
7. ___ Musket	E. A gun introduced in the 16th century, a precursor to the modern rifle
8. ___ Passel	F. A crudely built cabin or shack
9. ___ Shanty	G. A house for the person in charge of a canal lock
	H. A hissing sound made while frying
	I. A large group of people or things

Vocabulary:

Use a word from the box below to replace the underlined word or phrase in each sentence. Write your answer on the line provided.

1. The hash browns <u>hissed</u> in the hot grease in the frying pan. _____

2. Water rushed through the <u>canal gateway</u> to raise the water level so the boat could pass through. _____

3. Alexa and Austin <u>argued</u> about who had to wash the dishes. _____

4. The men in the militia were issued <u>guns</u> to perform training exercises. _____

5. The man in charge of the lock left his <u>house</u> to let a barge through the canal. _____

6. The "Old Lady in the Shoe" had a <u>ton</u> of children. _____

7. The <u>mules</u> pulled the heavy barge down the canal. _____

8. Slaves often lived in <u>shacks</u> on a plantation. _____

9. The <u>person slightly known</u> to Austin was a good friend of Alexa's. _____

Draft Animals	Bickered	Muskets	Acquaintance
Lock	Passel	Sizzled	Lock House
	Shanties		

Dark Enough to See the Stars Study Guide

Story Questions

1. What animals attacked Moses and Tillie on the towpath?

2. Who was Daniel Hughes?

3. Who did Moses hit in the face and why?

4. Where was the hiding place in Daniel Hughes' house?

5. Who was Katy Jane and how did she help runaways?

Discussion Questions

1. Do you think the trip was more dangerous for Tillie than for Moses? Why?

2. Why do you think Tillie didn't want Daniel Hughes to know that Jeb kissed her?

3. Define the word *superstition*. Was Tillie being superstitious when she put garlic on the pantry door? Why or why not?

4. Daniel Hughes said Katy Jane would rather live with wild animals than white plantation folk. Why?

Social Studies Connection

Learn more about canals and their use in 19th century America. Use the library and the Internet to discover why canals were important, how they worked, and what mode of transportation slowly replaced them. Read about the most famous American canal, the Erie Canal. Listen to the Erie Canal song: https://www.youtube.com/watch?v=HcNJ2RMOd3U

Writing Activity

Write about a specific superstition. Tell why you think it can't be true.

Chapters 24 - 30

Vocabulary:

Write the letter of the definition next to the correct vocabulary word.

1. ___ Half-Breed	A. A narrow walkway
2. ___ Logjam	B. An unflattering term for a person whose parents are of different races, especially Indian and white
3. ___ Buckskin	
4. ___ Callus	C. The skin of a deer
5. ___ Satchel	D. A religious meeting held in a tent or the open air
6. ___ Camp Meeting	E. Showy clothing and jewelry for dressing up
7. ___ Finery	F. A small purse or sack, sometimes having a shoulder strap
8. ___ Curtsy	G. A pile of tangled logs
9. ___ Gangway	H. A hardened part of skin, especially on hands and feet
10. ___ Gunnysack	I. A rough sack made of burlap
	J. A woman's respectful bow made by bending the knees and lowering the body

Vocabulary:

Use a word from the box below to replace the underlined word or phrase in each sentence. Write your answer on the line provided.

1. In the Old West, <u>people of mixed Indian and white descent</u> had a difficult time fitting in with either culture. _____

2. The <u>jumbled-up logs</u> blocked boats from sailing on the river. _____

3. The Indian princess wore a dress made out of <u>deerskins</u>. _____

4. Alex developed <u>tough skin</u> on his hands from working in the garden. _____

5. The country doctor carried a <u>bag</u> with his tools when he made house calls. _____

6. The weather was hot when the preacher taught at <u>an outdoor meeting</u> this summer. _____

7. The ladies dressed in their <u>exquisite gowns</u> to attend the gala celebrity event. _____

Dark Enough to See the Stars Study Guide

8. The duchess <u>bowed</u> before the Queen of England. _____

9. We carefully walked up the <u>narrow walkway</u> and boarded the ship. _____

10. The miller filled the <u>burlap sack</u> with cornmeal. _____

Half-Breeds	Gunnysack	Logjam	Gangway
Calluses	Curtsied	Satchel	Camp Meeting
	Finery		

Story Questions

1. Who was John Montour and how did he help Moses and Tillie?
_____
_____

2. What did John Montour give Mose?
_____
_____

3. In Ithaca, where did Pastor Loguen hide Moses and Tillie?
_____
_____

4. What did George teach Moses to do on the way to Cayuga Lake?
_____
_____

5. Why did Moses and Tillie have to hide in the cargo hold?
_____
_____

6. While they were in the hold, what did Moses promise God and why?
_____
_____

Dark Enough to See the Stars Study Guide

Discussion Question

1. Jervis warned Dr. Smith to be careful about doctoring people in Slabtown. Why?

___

2. Jervis told the doctor, "Whatever cargo you've got for Rochester, you'd better ship quickly." What did he really mean, and why did he use those terms?

___

3. John Jones told George Johnson they were afraid "slavery sympathizers" may have heard the church bell ring. Why do you think not everyone in the North was against slavery?

___

4. When they were in the cargo hold, Moses had second thoughts about choosing to run away. He even wondered if the white preacher was right about God creating black people to serve whites. Have you ever wondered if something you believe to be right is actually wrong?

___

Social Studies Connection

Research the Sheshequin Indian Trail. Do you think any Indian trails eventually became roads?

___

Writing Activity

Moses and Tillie felt scared in the cargo hold. Write a paragraph about something that scared you.

Chapters 31 - 34

Vocabulary:

Write the letter of the definition next to the correct vocabulary word.

1. ___ Huddle	A. Bedding that can be rolled up and carried from place to place
2. ___ Stationmaster	B. An idea
3. ___ Respectable	C. Crowd together closely
4. ___ Notion	D. The owner of a house used to help slaves on the Underground Railroad
5. ___ Neigh	
6. ___ Chaw	E. To close the hands or teeth tightly
7. ___ Bedroll	F. To be admired
8. ___ Clench	G. To wrinkle up the lips
9. ___ Pucker	H. A piece of chewing tobacco
	I. The sound a horse makes; whinny

Vocabulary:

Use a word from the box below to replace the underlined word or phrase in each sentence. Write your answer on the line provided.

1. The football players gathered together to discuss the next play. _____

2. Frederick Douglass was a shop owner who housed slaves on the Underground Railroad. _____

3. The horse whinnied when he saw the rattlesnake. _____

4. Alexa wrinkled her lips when she tasted the sour lemon. _____

5. Austin tightly balled his fists in anger when they lost the football game. _____

6. The cowboy unrolled his blankets next to the campfire and went to sleep. _____

7. The cowboy spit out his chewing tobacco before he went to sleep. _____

8. Austin's mom asked, "Whoever gave you the idea that you could play outside before you finished your homework?" _____

9. Alexa's dad said that being a policeman was a <u>worthy</u> occupation. _____

Clenched	Chaw	Huddled	Puckered
Respectable	Notion	Bedroll	Neighed
	Stationmaster		

Story Questions

1. Where did Moses and Tillie hide on the train?
_____
_____

2. Where did Frederick Douglass say they were to spend the night?
_____

3. Who showed up when Moses and Tillie rode to where they were supposed to stay?
_____
_____

4. How did Moses and Tillie escape?
_____
_____

5. When a gun fired and Moses and Tillie heard the words "He's dead," what was Moses afraid would happen?
_____
_____

6. Moses and Tillie were riding on what kind of road? What did they have to do to travel on this road?
_____
_____
_____

Discussion Questions

1. Why did Moses say he was riding a freedom train? How did that differ from the train on which his mama rode?

2. Aaron, one of the slave catchers, was a black man. Why do you think a black man would capture his own kind and return them to slavery? What might be his motives?

3. People who worked on the Underground Railroad risked their lives to help slaves become free. Why do you think they put themselves in danger? Can you think of anyone today who risks his or her life for others?

4. "What is possible for me is possible for you. Believe in yourself and take advantage of every opportunity." This sentence from Chapter 32 is an actual quote from Frederick Douglass. Could this quote be used in a history book? Why or why not? Remember, history books give facts. They are non-fiction. Could anything that Moses said in *Dark Enough to See the Stars* be used in a history book? Why or why not?

Social Studies Connection

The motto for Frederick Douglass' newspaper, *The North Star*, was "Right is of no sex—Truth is of no color—God is the Father of us all, and we are all brethren." Research this newspaper and discuss what Frederick Douglass meant by this statement. Did he champion the rights of anyone besides black people?

_____
_____

Literary Device: Cliff-Hanger

A cliff-hanger is a moment of increased tension or suspense at the end of an episode or chapter to encourage the reader to continue reading. You leave your character hanging off the edge of a cliff, so to speak. What was the cliff-hanger in chapter 33? Have you found any other cliff-hangers in the story so far?

_____
_____
_____
_____

Writing Activity

Write a paragraph about what you think Frederick Douglass meant by: "What is possible for me is possible for you. Believe in yourself and take advantage of every opportunity."

_____
_____
_____
_____
_____
_____
_____

Chapters 35 - 38

Vocabulary:

Determine the meaning of the following words by the context in the following sentences. Then compare your definition with the dictionary definition.

1. Jeb pulled a pair of *shackles* out of his saddlebag and put them around Tillie's wrists.

    Your definition:

    Dictionary definition:

2. I ran up next to that black traitor lying under his horse. A *Judas*—that's what he was.

    Your definition:

    Dictionary definition:

3. Jeb *trussed* up Tillie with a rope like she was a deer.

    Your definition:

    Dictionary definition:

4. Jeb *cackled* with glee when he caught Tillie.

    Your definition:

_____

_____

    Dictionary definition:

_____

_____

5. The rope yanked around Jeb's arm like a hangman's *noose*.

    Your definition:

_____

_____

    Dictionary definition:

_____

_____

6. Tillie and Moses walked across the bridge as *pedestrians*.

    Your definition:

_____

_____

    Dictionary definition:

_____

_____

7. Moses feared that the stable boy at the stagecoach company was in *cahoots* with the slave catchers, Jeb and Aaron.

    Your definition:

_____

_____

    Dictionary definition:

_____

_____

8. Charlie loaded bags in the hold of the stagecoach while Phil, the driver, checked the *tack and traces* on the three horses.

    Your definition:

    Dictionary definition:

9. Tillie *clambered* over the stagecoach railing and lay next to Moses.

    Your definition:

    Dictionary definition:

Story Questions

1. Where did Shadow take the buggy and why?

2. Dan heard Moses and Tillie tell Mr. Fanning some terrible news. What was it?

3. Why did Dan leave work and go to Rochester?

Dark Enough to See the Stars Study Guide

4. What kind of bridge spanned the Niagara River?

5. Why wouldn't Moses leave Tillie?

6. At the Free Soil Hotel, who invited Moses to come home with him?

7. What did Moses write for *The Voice of the Fugitive* newspaper? Why did he write it?

Discussion Questions

1. Freedom isn't free. Someone always pays a price. What characters in this book paid a price for freedom? How did they do that?

2. Moses started out with a dream. He dreamed he could be free from slavery. His mama planted that dream in him from an early age. As he ran toward freedom, another dream formed within him—the hope that he could someday be an abolitionist writer. After he accomplished his dream of freedom from slavery, he had a dream for someone else—that he might help his mother become free. Do you think it's important to have a dream? Can you have more than one dream?

_____
_____
_____
_____

Literary Device: Foreshadowing

Foreshadowing is a technique that authors use to give clues or warnings about what will happen later in the story. In this section, what hints does the author give that there is trouble ahead?

_____
_____
_____
_____

Writing Activity

Write about your dreams. Do you have more than one dream? Is anyone helping you accomplish your dreams?

_____
_____
_____
_____
_____
_____

Underground Railroad and Dark Enough to See the Stars Exam

The following exam has two sections. The first section tests the students' knowledge of Underground Railroad history as presented in my novel and study guide. The second section tests the students' knowledge of the novel and Moses' story.

Section 1: Underground Railroad History Exam

Instructions:

Circle all the answers that apply. Many questions have more than one answer.

1. What was the Underground Railroad?

    a. A railroad that carried goods from Albany to Buffalo, New York
    b. A system of people and places that helped people escape from slavery
    c. A passenger train between Pennsylvania and Canada
    d. An underground railroad that slaves dug to help them escape

2. When was the Underground Railroad active?

    a. During the 1900s
    b. During the 1800s
    c. During the 1600s
    d. During the 1500s

3. What was the Big Dipper?

    a. A ladle slaves used to drink water
    b. A constellation
    c. A group of stars known as an asterism
    d. A dance from the 1800s

4. Why did slaves call the Big Dipper the "Drinking Gourd?"

    a. Because it reminded them of a song
    b. Because that was its scientific name
    c. Because it looked like a ladle for dipping water
    d. Because the Indians called it that

5. Why was the Big Dipper important to slaves?

    a. The light from its stars helped them find their way in the dark
    b. It pointed to the North Star which helped them know how to go north
    c. They used it to get a drink of water
    d. It helped them understand the constellations

6. What was the Mason-Dixon Line?

    a. The boundary line between Pennsylvania and Maryland
    b. The boundary line between New York and Canada
    c. A railroad that carried slaves on the Underground Railroad
    d. A boundary line between the North and the South

7. Who was Thaddeus Stevens?

    a. A United States congressman
    b. A teacher
    c. A freed slave
    d. An abolitionist who helped slaves

8. What was the Fugitive Slave Act of 1850?

    a. A law made by Congress
    b. Required Northerners to return escaped slaves to the South
    c. Gave permission for slaves to stay in the North
    d. Punished people who helped escaped slaves

9. Who was Daniel Hughes?

    a. An escaped slave
    b. A canal boat captain
    c. A state senator
    d. A half black, half Indian man

10. Who was Frederick Douglass?

    a. An abolitionist
    b. A writer who wrote about the wrongs of slavery
    c. An escaped slave
    d. A white man who helped slaves escape

11. What was the North Star publication?

    a. A book
    b. A newspaper
    c. A song
    d. A poem

12. Who was Henry Bibb?

    a. An abolitionist
    b. An escaped slave
    c. A newspaper publisher
    d. An author

13. What was the name of Henry Bibb's newspaper?

    a. The Canada Times
    b. The Bibb Gazette
    c. Freedom's Choice
    d. The Voice of the Fugitive

14. Why did slaves travel to Canada?

    a. They liked the cold weather
    b. They could find work there
    c. Slavery was illegal in Canada
    d. The Fugitive Slave Act made it dangerous to live in America

Section 2: Dark Enough to See the Stars Exam

Instructions:

Circle all the answers that apply. Many questions have more than one answer.

1. Why did Moses run away from the plantation?

    a. He didn't want to be a slave anymore
    b. He had to leave his mama, who was going to be sold away
    c. He wanted to go visit a friend in another state
    d. He wanted to be a sailor on a schooner

2. Who taught Moses to write his name?

    a. Miller Johnson
    b. Daniel Morgan
    c. Joel
    d. Miz Oakley

3. At the Dobbin House, where was the hidey-hole located?

    a. In the cellar
    b. In the outhouse
    c. Next to the kitchen
    d. In the wall next to the staircase

4. Who wrote the free paper for Moses?

    a. Thaddeus Stevens
    b. Matthew Dobbin
    c. Miller Johnson
    d. Henry Butler

5. Where did Moses first meet Tillie?

    a. At the mill
    b. At Reverend Palmer's house
    c. At Dr. Rutherford's office
    d. At the Dobbin House

6. What kind of boat did Daniel Hughes own?

    a. A steamboat
    b. A row boat
    c. A canal boat
    d. A schooner

7. Why did Moses hit Daniel Hughes' hired hand, Jeb?

    a. Jeb attacked Moses
    b. Jeb called Daniel Hughes bad names
    c. Jeb was stealing cash from Daniel Hughes
    d. Jeb kissed Tillie without her permission

8. Who was John Montour?

    a. A United States congressman
    b. A part Iroquois Indian fur trapper
    c. The man who led Moses and Tillie through the woods to Dr. Nathaniel Smith's house
    d. A doctor in Elmira

9. What kind of boat did Captain Buckbee own?

    a. A steamboat
    b. A rowboat
    c. A canal boat
    d. A schooner

10. Why did Moses and Tillie stay in the cargo hold?

    a. It was the most comfortable place to stay
    b. They needed to hide from slave catchers
    c. Captain Buckbee told them to stay there
    d. Jeb had followed them onto the boat

11. What did Frederick Douglass tell Tillie?

    a. "Please cook me breakfast."
    b. "Girls need to know their place."
    c. "I'm very impressed with your schooling."
    d. "Every young lady should be educated. Don't let anyone tell you otherwise."

12. What did Frederick Douglass tell Moses?

    a. "What is possible for me is possible for you. Believe in yourself and take advantage of every opportunity."
    b. "Moses, someday you may write an article for this paper."
    c. "I will train you to work in my print shop."
    d. "Don't dream too big. You might be disappointed."

13. What river did Moses and Tillie need to cross to reach Canada?

    a. The Missouri River
    b. The Delaware River
    c. The Niagara River
    d. The Mississippi River

14. Why did Tillie jump off the bridge?

    a. She never really wanted to go to Canada
    b. She knew how to swim
    c. Jeb had tied her up. She didn't want to go back with him
    d. She wanted to help Moses escape, even though she could not escape

15. Who helped Moses in Canada?

    a. The Niagara bridge toll keeper
    b. The owner of the Free Soil Hotel
    c. Henry Bibb
    d. Tom Sawyer

16. What did Moses do in Canada?

    a. He learned how to read and write at Miz Bibb's school
    b. He learned how to ride a horse
    c. He wrote a letter to his mom that was printed in Henry Bibb's paper
    d. He learned how to be a blacksmith

Dark Enough to See the Stars Answer Key

Answers to the "Before You Read the Book" section

1. This story is about a twelve-year-old boy who runs away from his plantation home and travels on the Underground Railroad to find freedom from slavery.

2. History books are about actual events. Authors must intensively research their subject and follow the timeline of history. They may only use dialogue originally used by the people they are writing about. This can be found in letters, court records, videos, or recordings.

Fiction writers must also research the era about which they write. Historical facts should not be changed to suit the author's story. Rather, the writer constructs fictional characters whose personalities and stories fit in with the facts of the time. Historical fiction writers often include figures from history in their account. The author of Dark Enough to See the Stars writes about Frederick Douglass, his newspaper, print shop, and staff. The author uses a partial quote of an actual statement Douglass made, and fits it into the fictional dialogue. The following blog discusses the difference between nonfiction, creative non-fiction, and historical fiction.[1]

3. Historical fiction not only informs, it entertains. It also gives the reader insight into the thoughts, feelings, and desires that people of that time may have experienced. This gives the reader understanding on an emotional as well as intellectual level.

4. Studying history gives us perspective. We learn that diverse cultures have different belief systems which may not agree with our own. We also learn what choices and actions people made in the past and what consequences, good or bad, resulted. With slavery and Underground Railroad history, the reader gains a perspective about the black experience in America, which can help foster understanding between the races and promote racial reconciliation. Comprehending our past can influence our beliefs.

5. Moses traveled approximately 400 miles to reach Niagara Falls, Canada. We could travel this distance in about six to seven hours by car. This trip took Moses about three months.

---

[1] http://www.donnajanellbowman.com/2010/08/25/nonfiction-vs-creative-nonfiction-vs-historical-fiction/

Chapters 1 – 4

DIALECT

1. **so's** — so that, so is, so as
2. **gonna** — going to
3. **ain't** — am not, are not, is not, has not, or have not
4. **goin'** — going
5. **outta** — out of
6. **catched** — caught
7. **knowed** — knew
8. **growed** — grew
9. **Masta** — Master
10. **whupped** — whipped
11. **gits** — gets
12. **forgit** — forget
13. **jus'** — just
14. **cipher** — old-fashioned word for arithmetic
15. **po'** — poor
16. **innards** — internal organs of the body

Vocabulary Matching

1. Kindling — A
2. Bulrush — L
3. Cowcatcher — K
4. Depot — M
5. Ruckus — J
6. Gully — G
7. Lash — H
8. Beau — B
9. Whittling — D
10. Squabbling — C
11. Tinker — E
12. Conductor — I
13. Yowling — F
14. Agent — N

Fill in the Blanks

1. Squabbling
2. Kindling
3. Depot
4. Yowling
5. Ruckus
6. Gully
7. Cowcatcher
8. Whittling
9. Beau
10. Conductor
11. Agent

Story Questions

1. She didn't want him to be a slave. She wanted him to escape like Moses did.
2. The slaves called the North Star the Drinking Gourd
3. Moses felt that Zeke was too young to make the dangerous trip.
4. She worked as a seamstress and made ball gowns.
5. The skunk threw the bloodhounds off his scent so they chased a deer instead.
6. He felt awkward and maybe ashamed because he was wet, dirty, and smelly.

Chapters 5 – 8

Vocabulary Matching

1. Hitched   B
2. Hopper   G
3. Burlap   D
4. Whitewash   A
5. Hunkered   H
6. Grits   E
7. Vittles   F
8. Tick   C
9. Impudent   I

Fill in the Blanks

1. Burlap
2. Vittles
3. Hunkered
4. Impudent
5. Whitewash
6. Grits
7. Hitched
8. Hopper

Story Questions

1. The millstones looked like two big lips smacking, and he felt he might be their next meal.

2. Miller Johnson was taking him to Gettysburg in a wagon. Moses had to hide because he was a runaway and could get captured if found.

3. The letter M was two mountains, O was a wheel, S looked like a snake, E resembled a ladder with one side missing.

4. Daniel kicked the cat because it scratched his arm.

5. Moses scratched his name on the loft floor to show that his name was special. He hoped other runaways would scratch their names too, to show that they were special.

Chapters 9 – 12

Vocabulary Matching:

1. Mosey   B
2. Buckboard   G
3. Flatbed   E
4. Bandanna   C
5. Kinfolk   D
6. Snuffling   A
7. Abolitionist   F

Vocabulary:

1. Moseyed
2. Buckboard
3. Flatbed
4. Bandanna
5. Abolitionists
6. Kinfolk
7. Snuffling

Story Questions

1. This wagon had a false bottom where he could hide.
2. They were going to Gettysburg.
3. They were crossing the Mason-Dixon Line, which separated slave states from free states.
4. The hidey-hole was a small room with a secret panel in a staircase wall.
5. Thaddeus Stevens was a lawyer and congressman. He wrote Moses a free paper.
6. Moses did not have to hide on the trip to Harrisburg because he had his free paper in his pocket.

Literary Device: Imagery

1. Smell
2. Touch
3. Touch
4. Sight

Dark Enough to See the Stars Study Guide
Chapters 13 – 18

Vocabulary Matching
1. Hightail   H
2. Clack   E
3. Whoop   A
4. Clomp   J
5. Militia   B
6. Brandish   K
7. Plunk   D
8. Sideboard   F
9. Dodge   G
10. Gumption   I
11. Towpath   C

Vocabulary:
1. Hightailed
2. Towpath
3. Plunked
4. Clacked
5. Gumption
6. Sideboard
7. Brandished
8. Militias
9. Dodged
10. Whooped
11. Clomped

Story Questions

1. Moses' free paper was ruined.

2. They said that Tillie could say he was her brother who was there to help harvest the crops.

3. Offenders were fined one thousand dollars and had to spend six months in jail for each slave they helped.

4. Moses wanted to be a writer for an abolitionist newspaper.

5. Moses and Tillie had to leave because the sheriff was coming to send them back to their owners.

Dark Enough to See the Stars Study Guide

Chapters 19-23

Vocabulary Matching:

1. Draft Animal   B
2. Bicker   A
3. Acquaintance   D
4. Lock   C
5. Lock House   G
6. Sizzle   H
7. Musket   E
8. Passel   I
9. Shanty   F

Vocabulary:

1. Sizzled
2. Lock
3. Bickered
4. Muskets
5. Lock House
6. Passel
7. Draft Animals
8. Shanties
9. Acquaintance

Story Questions

1. Wolves attacked Tillie and Moses.

2. Daniel Hughes was a canal boat captain who was half black and half Indian.

3. Moses hit Jeb because he kissed Tillie without her permission.

4. The Hugheses' had a secret hiding place in the pantry.

5. Katy Jane was a former slave who lived on a mountain and warned runaways by flashing one lantern if slave catchers were nearby. She flashed two if it was safe to go.

Dark Enough to See the Stars Study Guide

Chapters 24 – 30

Vocabulary Matching

1. Half-Breed   B
2. Logjam   G
3. Satchel   F
4. Camp Meeting D
5. Fineries   E
6. Curtsy   J
7. Gangway   A
8. Gunnysack   I

Vocabulary:

1. Half-Breeds
2. Logjam
3. Buckskin
4. Calluses
5. Satchel
6. Camp Meeting
7. Finery
8. Curtsied
9. Gangway
10. Gunnysack

Story Questions

1. John Montour was a trapper who was part Iroquois Indian. He accompanied Moses and Tillie on the Sheshequin Indian Trail from Williamsport, Pennsylvania, to Elmira, New York.

2. John gave Moses his hunting knife.

3. Pastor Loguen hid Moses and Tillie in the top of a bell tower.

4. George taught Moses how to drive a horse and buggy.

5. Moses and Tillie had to hide in the hold because they saw that the slave catcher Jeb was on the boat looking for them.

6. Moses promised God he would do whatever God wanted if he and Tillie escaped alive.

Dark Enough to See the Stars Study Guide

CHAPTERS 31 - 34

Vocabulary Matching

1. Huddle   C
2. Stationmaster D
3. Respectable   F
4. Notion   B
5. Neigh   I
6. Chaw   H
7. Bedroll   A
8. Clench   E
9. Pucker   G

Vocabulary:

1. Huddle
2. Stationmaster
3. Neighed
4. Puckered
5. Clenched
6. Bedroll
7. Chaw
8. Notion
9. Respectable

Story Questions

1. They hid in the baggage car.
2. They were supposed to spend the night at Joseph Post's house.
3. Two slave catchers, Jeb and Aaron, showed up.
4. They escaped in the buggy when Joseph Post slapped the horse with his hat.
5. If the slave catchers came after them, Moses was afraid he and Tillie would be blamed for the death.
6. They were on a toll road and had to pay money to go on it.

Dark Enough to See the Stars Study Guide

Chapters 35 – 38

Story Questions

1. Shadow took the buggy to the T.W. Fanning Stagecoach Company of Lockport, New York, because that was the horse's original home.

2. Moses and Tillie told Mr. Fanning that slave catchers stopped their buggy as they were approaching Joseph Post's house for shelter. When Joseph Post smacked the horse so it would run away, Moses and Tillie heard shots fired behind them. They also heard that someone was dead, and it might have been Jeb or Aaron.

3. Dan was Aaron's brother. He left to find out if his brother was dead.

4. A suspension bridge spanned the Niagara River.

5. Moses couldn't let Tillie face Jeb alone. It would have haunted him the rest of his life.

6. Henry Bibb took Moses home with him.

7. Moses wrote a letter to his mama. He wanted to tell her he was a free person in Canada, and he hoped the letter would help him find his mama.

Underground Railroad and *Dark Enough to See the Stars* Exam Answer Key

Underground Railroad Exam

1. b
2. b
3. c
4. c
5. b
6. a, d
7. a, d
8. a, b, d
9. b, d
10. a, b, c
11. b
12. a, b, c, d
13. d
14. c, d

Dark Enough to See the Stars Exam

1. a, b
2. c
3. d
4. a
5. b
6. c
7. d
8. b, c
9. a
10. b, d
11. c, d
12. a, b
13. c
14. c, d
15. a, b, c
16. a, c

About the Author

Cindy Noonan's expert knowledge of Underground Railroad history in Pennsylvania, New York, and Canada gives authenticity to *Dark Enough to See the Stars*. Through the eyes of her novel, readers receive insight into the people who helped slaves escape, the places where slaves hid, and the transportation they used on their trek to freedom.

Cindy has recently launched an online women's ministry called Embrace Your Destiny to help women fulfill the callings on their lives, much as her protagonist, Moses, fulfills his. She resides in Northeast Pennsylvania with her husband of fifty years, Frank. After raising five children, they now enjoy time with their ten grandchildren.

Cindy can be contacted at Cindy@cindynoonan.com.

www.ingramcontent.com/pod-product-compliance
Lightning Source LLC
Chambersburg PA
CBHW060427010526
44118CB00017B/2395